"Echoes of Empty Pockets"

Author: Samel Karki

This book contains varying degrees of the following:
Insert appropriate content warnings here.
Please read safely and responsibly.

"ECHOES OF EMPTY POCKETS"

Introduction

Dear readers,

I extend my warmest gratitude to all of you for granting me this invaluable opportunity to introduce myself. My name is Samel Karki, and I am delighted to embark on this journey with you through the pages of my book.

As we venture into this literary voyage together, I would like to extend a heartfelt greeting to each and every one of you. Regardless of where you are in the world, I hope my words find you in good health and high spirits. May this book serve as a source of inspiration, knowledge, and joy for you, just as writing it has been a fulfilling and rewarding experience for me.

In this book, we will delve into unique, genuine, and essential concepts that are imperative for us to grasp in our lives. During my younger age, I focused on learning survival skills for navigating the world, understanding the importance of education, grasping the concepts of debit and credit, and different laws, all imparted by my schools and colleges. I believe that most individuals went through similar educational experiences, which prepared us for a middle-class existence. The emphasis was on excelling academically, securing good jobs, and establishing a career – a perspective largely limited to a middle-class mindset.

Undoubtedly, the knowledge acquired from schools and colleges bears great significance in shaping our lives. Nevertheless, given the context of today's highly advanced technological age, there emerges a pressing need to broaden our comprehension. Questions arise: What exactly is Financial Education? How do we define genuine success?

How can we achieve mastery over the discipline of money and fathom its intricate workings? Moreover, it becomes imperative to recognize the intricate dynamics that govern our relationships with family, friends, and relatives, particularly when faced with financial adversities.

In the present day, we are fortunate to have access to institutions that provide financial education, along with proficient advisors in school and university sectors, coupled with a plethora of information available on social media platforms. Regrettably, these resources often come with a high cost. As a result, those who are financially capable stand a higher chance of achieving success.

Conversely, those who lack the means to access such opportunities may find themselves ensnared in a cycle of poverty. This cycle can lead to a persistent middle-class existence marked by debts and daily financial struggles. Tragically, this pattern has the potential to endure across generations, further deepening the divide between financial classes.

To those who come from middle-class families, there's no need to worry. As the pages of this book unfold, we will reveal strategies that have the potential to pave the way for a reimagined future – a future characterized by prosperity achieved through well-guided steps.

A Little Introduction About Myself: Originally hailing from the beautiful country of Nepal, I have been fortunate to have a life enriched with diverse experiences. In 2016, destiny led me to the Middle East, "Now, with a heart full of belonging and joy, I can confidently call this place 'home'. These years in the Middle East have been instrumental in shaping my perspectives, broadening my horizons, and allowing me to witness the tapestry of life from a unique vantage point.
At the age of 28, I find myself standing at the threshold of endless possibilities, eager to share my thoughts, ideas, and stories with all of you. This book serves as a culmination of my passions and aspirations, and I hope it leaves an indelible mark on your hearts.

Once again, I extend my heartfelt gratitude for joining me on this adventure. Let us embark on this literary journey together, where the power of words knows no bounds, and the magic of storytelling awaits us.

A Special Thanks to my dear wife Sanu maya Karki:

I am beyond grateful for the incredible support of my wife and the love she has shown me during my challenging financial times. Her unwavering presence by my side, coupled with her genuine smile and boundless love, have been a source of my strength.

In the face of adversity, she has never once shown any anger or frustration towards me. Her love has transformed the hardest times into opportunities for growth and togetherness. I am incredibly lucky to have you as my life partner, and I promise to cherish, protect, and love you for all eternity. Thank you, my dear wife, for being the rock in my life and for providing me with the warmth of your love and unwavering support. I am forever grateful to you.

Thanks,
Samel Karki

Title: Echoes of Empty Pockets.

Index

Section I: Navigating Empty Pockets in a World Without Wealth.

As I write this book, I find myself pondering the mystery of my ability to do so. Yet, amidst the creative flow, I cannot turn a blind eye to the prevailing financial crises of our time. I witness many from my generation losing their jobs, struggling without clear goals or plans for their lives. Reminiscing about my youth, I too lacked the guidance of a financial advisor. Together, let us explore the pages of this book, seeking understanding and perhaps finding a path towards a brighter financial future.

In a world where material wealth often defines the dynamics of human relationships, the notion "No money, everyone will be your enemy" strikes a profound chord. As I explore this captivating topic, I aim to shed light on the intricate connections between finances and friendship, the role of wealth in forging social bonds, and the impact it has on our lives.

This poignant statement reflects the harsh reality that financial constraints can sometimes alienate us from the very essence of companionship. I invite you to join me on this thought-provoking journey as I unravel the reasons behind this phenomenon and contemplate its implications on our society and personal well-being.

In the below pages, I shall unravel the layers of this concept, exploring the reasons why lack of monetary resources may lead to social isolation. Through insightful anecdotes, compelling research, and introspective analysis, I aspire to not only comprehend the roots of this issue but also to instigate meaningful conversations about the true essence of friendship beyond financial boundaries.

Let us embark together on this quest for understanding, compassion, and empathy, as we confront the profound implications of "No money, everyone will be your enemy." By the end of this exploration, may we discover the timeless virtues of genuine friendship that transcend the constraints of wealth, nurturing a deeper sense of connection and camaraderie among us all.

Section II: Understanding the Effects of Financial Difficulties.

In a world where economic uncertainties and financial challenges have become increasingly prevalent, the impact of financial difficulties on individuals and societies cannot be ignored. From unexpected job losses to mounting debts and dwindling savings, countless people find themselves caught in the web of financial strain, facing a wide array of consequences that extend far beyond the realm of money.

This Book delves into the profound effects of financial difficulties, shedding light on the multifaceted aspects of this pervasive issue. By exploring the psychological, emotional, and social repercussions of financial struggles, we aim to provide a comprehensive understanding of how financial difficulties can permeate every facet of a person's life.

Beyond the surface-level numbers and statistics, this Book delves into the human stories behind financial hardships. From the sleepless nights and strained relationships to the self-esteem challenges and mental health implications, we strive to paint a vivid picture of the human toll that financial difficulties exact on those affected.

Moreover, we will examine the broader societal impact of financial woes, as they ripple through communities and economies, potentially leading to increased poverty, reduced access to education and healthcare, and exacerbating inequality. By grasping the interconnectedness of individual financial struggles and their repercussions on society, we can better appreciate the urgency of addressing these issues collectively.

However, this Book is not merely a disheartening account of financial woes. In recognizing the significance of understanding the effects of financial difficulties, we also aim to highlight the resilience and coping mechanisms individuals and communities employ during challenging times. By drawing on inspirational stories of triumph over adversity, we aspire to offer readers a sense of hope and encouragement.

Throughout the pages of this Book, we shall explore practical strategies for navigating financial difficulties, managing stress and anxiety, and seeking support when needed. Armed with knowledge and insights, we believe that individuals can develop the tools to weather financial storms more effectively and emerge stronger on the other side.

In conclusion, "Understanding the Effects of Financial Difficulties" is an exploration of the profound impact that financial struggles have on the lives of individuals and the fabric of societies. It aims to foster empathy, awareness, and actionable knowledge for those facing financial challenges and those who wish to support them. As we embark on this journey of understanding, let us approach the subject with compassion and a commitment to making a positive difference in the lives of those who bear the weight of financial burdens.

Section III: The Psychology of Enmity in Times of Scarcity.

In times of scarcity, when the purse strings tighten and resources dwindle, the psychology of enmity comes to the forefront, unraveling complex emotions and behaviors that can turn friends into foes and neighbors into adversaries. As the desperation to secure limited resources intensifies, the human psyche undergoes a profound transformation, compelling individuals to view others with suspicion and competition, perceiving them as potential threats to their survival.

The scarcity mindset takes hold, engendering a "survival of the fittest" mentality, where the quest for limited resources morphs into a battleground for dominance, fostering deep-rooted feelings of animosity towards those who may stand in the way.

In the face of scarcity, social dynamics shift, and once harmonious communities can fracture into factions, each vying fiercely for a slice of the dwindling pie, leaving little. In the realm of scarcity, even minor disagreements can escalate into bitter feuds, as the scarcity mindset fuels a zero-sum outlook, where any gain by one party is perceived as a loss by another, deepening the chasm of enmity between them.

As the pages of this Book unfold, we delve into the intricate workings of the human psyche during times of scarcity, unravelling the multifaceted nature of enmity and shedding light on the potential pathways to transcend it. By exploring psychological insights and practical strategies, we hope to illuminate the transformative power of empathy and collaboration, offering a beacon of hope amidst the darkness of scarcity-induced enmity.

Section IV: The Challenges of Living Without Money.

Living without money presents a myriad of daunting challenges, as it forces individuals to navigate a world that revolves around financial transactions and economic exchanges.

Imagine a pocket with a hole, just as the contents of that pocket slip away unnoticed, so too can our relationships unravel when plagued by the erosion of trust and support. Picture a world where these relationships are like stars in the night sky-each one a luminous point of connection. Yet, when the fabric of our emotions becomes threadbare, and our pockets of trust develop holes, those stars dim, and connections grow distant.

In the realm of family, where blood ties are thought to be unbreakable, a torn pocket can unveil unsettling truths. But it's not just family ties that feel the impact of these holes. Friendships, those beautiful wildflowers that bloom in the garden of companionship, can wither when the pocket of trust is left unstitched. The promises made, the laughter shared, all can be lost if those connections are taken for granted.

Living without money means relinquishing the comfort and convenience that financial stability provides, making even the simplest aspects of daily life, like transportation and communication, arduous challenges to overcome.

In a society where money serves as the lifeblood of daily existence, the absence of financial resources can render even the most basic needs, such as food, shelter, and healthcare, elusive and unattainable. Stripped of financial means, individuals must confront the harsh reality of social exclusion, as the lack of money often leads to marginalization and alienation from mainstream society.

Surviving without money demands exceptional resourcefulness and creativity, as individuals must devise alternative means of obtaining necessities, relying on bartering, sharing economies, and community support. Without money to buffer against life's uncertainties, the tiniest, unexpected expense can quickly snowball into a profound crisis, leaving individuals vulnerable to cascading hardships. The absence of money places immense strain on mental and emotional well-being, fostering feelings of powerlessness, anxiety, and despair, as individuals grapple with the constant pressure of survival.

Navigating legal and bureaucratic systems becomes an uphill battle, as many societal structures and services are designed around monetary transactions, leaving those without money struggling to access essential rights and privileges. Lack of money can lead to compromised physical health, as individuals may forgo necessary medical care and proper nutrition due to financial constraints, putting their well-being at significant risk.

Living without money often entails embracing a minimalist lifestyle, where possessions and material goods are pared down to the bare essentials, redefining what it means to find value and fulfillment in life. Despite the hardships, the challenges of living without money also offer glimpses of resilience and community solidarity, showcasing the strength of human connections and the potential for collective support in the face of adversity.

Throughout this Book, we delve deep into the daunting realities faced by those navigating life without money, examining the profound impact on various aspects of their lives and the societal structures that perpetuate such challenges.

By shedding light on the experiences of individuals living on the margins, we aim to foster empathy, awareness, and a call to action, inspiring readers to engage in meaningful discussions and seek solutions that pave the way towards a more equitable and compassionate world.

In the end, the lesson is clear: to maintain the vibrant mosaic of relationships, one must constantly examine and repair the pockets of trust that can erode over time. Only then can we prevent the stars of kinship and companionship from fading into distant constellations and ensure that we remain woven together as the fabric of shared humanity.

Dear readers,

Welcome to a journey. As we step into Chapter 1, prepare to be immersed in a world of intrigue, emotion, and discovery. Unfold the pages and let curiosity be your guide. Adventure awaits, so let's embark together.

Chapter 1
The real story about the cost of financial difficulty on our emotions.

Fragments of Fortune:

A Life of Stability
Introduce Samel, a diligent middle-aged man with a stable job, a loving family, and a comfortable lifestyle. He enjoys the simple pleasures of life. Samuel's financial situation is secure, and he believes that his family's happiness is anchored in their financial stability.

Shadows of Uncertainty
Unexpectedly, Samel's world takes an unexpected turn. A series of unfortunate events – a sudden job change, debts, and mounting bills – shatter his sense of security. He faces the harsh reality of job changes and dwindling savings, and his confidence begins to crumble. as financial stress takes a toll on his emotions, his friends and Family.

The Weight of Responsibility
He struggles to find a better job in a competitive market. As the primary breadwinner, he carries the weight of responsibility on his shoulders. The pressure to provide for his family causes his anxiety to escalate, affecting his sleep, and his ability to be present for his family. The emotional cost of financial difficulty becomes a heavy burden that he battles daily.

Fractured Connections

As Samel's financial situation deteriorates, he begins to withdraw from his social circles. He avoids gatherings with friends, feeling embarrassed by his inability to maintain his previous lifestyle. The isolation intensifies his emotional struggles, as he grapples with feelings of shame and inadequacy. His friends, unaware of his situation, begin to drift away.

Desperation and Despair

Despite having a good income compared to his friends, Samuel's difficulties increase day by day due to the weight of responsibility and debts he carries. He struggles to see a way out of his predicament, and his self-esteem plummets. He experiences moments of deep despair and questions why he cannot be a good husband and a good son. The emotional toll of his financial difficulties starts to overshadow his identity and sense of purpose.

Breaking point

Samel reaches a breaking point, realizing that the cost of his financial struggles extends far beyond himself – it's impacting the very core of his family's unity.

A Glimmer of Hope

Amidst the darkness, Samuel begins attending support groups for individuals facing financial difficulties. Through sharing his story and hearing others' experiences, he realizes he's not alone in his struggles. He learns practical strategies for managing stress and anxiety, and he starts rebuilding connections with his friends and family.

Reclaiming Emotions, Rebuilding Life

Samel's journey towards healing gains momentum. He enrolls in workshops to enhance his skills and expand his job prospects. As he secures a new job and takes small steps toward financial stability, he experiences a shift in his emotions. He discovers the importance of open communication with his wife, fostering resilience in their relationship.

Discovering True Value

Over time, he begins to redefine his perception of success and happiness. He realizes that his worth isn't solely tied to his financial status. The experiences he's endured have taught him to appreciate the emotional bonds he shares with his family and friends. He learns that his true value lies in the love and support he gives and receives.

New Beginnings

He emerges as a stronger, more empathetic individual. While scars from his financial hardships remain, he embraces his transformed perspective on life. He has become an advocate for mental health awareness within the context of financial struggles, using his story to inspire others to seek help and cultivate emotional well-being.

Epilogue: "Samel's Redemption" is a poignant tale that illuminates the hidden costs of financial difficulty on one's emotions and relationships. He hasn't fully recovered from his financial bad situation, but he has found a way and is slowly working on it. Through Samuel's journey, readers are reminded that adversity can lead to personal growth, increased resilience, and a deeper understanding of what truly matters in life. The story serves as an emotional roadmap for those navigating similar challenges, showing that even in the face of financial hardship, redemption and renewal are possible.

It's my own story, and I am Samel. I have mastered the way to earn money, how it works, what assets and liabilities are, what the right investments are, how to be free from debts, and many other things that I will describe to you in the chapters below.

Chapter 2

The Social Isolation and Judgment of the Stigma of Being Broke.

In a world where financial success often seems like a measure of personal worth, the experience of having empty pockets can extend far beyond the realm of financial difficulties.

In the shadows of bustling streets and opulent storefronts, a quiet struggle unfolds that transcends the mere absence of financial abundance. The experience of having empty pockets is a journey that traverses far beyond the realm of monetary hardship, infiltrating the deepest corners of an individual's psyche. It introduces a harsh dichotomy of social isolation and the weighty stigma that society attaches to financial adversity.

an invisible yet formidable force, casts its judgment upon those grappling with empty pockets. Society often paints these individuals with a broad brush, branding them as lacking ambition or responsibility. This branding extends beyond economic circumstances, seeping into their sense of self-worth and influencing the way they are perceived by others. The psychological burden becomes palpable as shame takes root, leaving these individuals trapped in a cycle of internalized blame and worthlessness.

But it's not just the internal struggle that plagues them; it's the isolation that festers in their interactions with the world around them. Friends and family, once close, can unknowingly contribute to this isolation by misunderstanding the complexities of financial hardship. Social events that once brought joy now become sources of anxiety as the fear of judgment looms large. In an age where social media showcases the curated highlights of others' lives, the stark contrast to their own can magnify feelings of inadequacy, pushing them further into the shadows of isolation.

Yet, within the narrative of struggle lies the power of resilience. Personal stories of individuals who have weathered the storm of empty pockets emerge as beacons of strength. These stories reveal the intersection of identity, where factors like race, gender, and background intersect with financial challenges, sometimes magnifying the isolation but also highlighting the unique facets of their journey.

While society's empathy deficit remains a challenge, there is a glimmer of hope. By challenging perceptions and fostering open conversations, we can foster understanding and break down the walls of isolation. Empowerment emerges from the sense of community that can be found in support groups, online forums, and local organizations, offering a lifeline to those who feel adrift.

In the end, "Empty Pockets: Navigating the Social Isolation and Stigma of Being Broke" is more than a book. It urges society to recognize the complex interplay between financial hardship, isolation, and stigma, and to work collectively to build a more inclusive world-one where an empty wallet does not equate to an empty sense of self.

Chapter 3

Unmasking Friendships: When Pockets Run Dry

Friendship, that seemingly intangible bond that weaves the fabric of our lives, often stands as a testament to our shared experiences, laughter, and memories. But as the pages of life turn, and the chapters unfold, the role of wealth and resources can emerge as an unanticipated character in this narrative. "Unmasking Friendships: When Pockets Run Dry" takes us on a journey through the labyrinthine alleys of human connections, exposing the intricate dynamics that arise when financial situations evolve and our pockets, once flush, now lie empty.

The Role of Money in Relationships, An Uncomfortable Truth:

In the world where we navigate relationships, be they familial, platonic, or romantic, money has a pervasive yet often unspoken role. The presence of abundance can veil the authenticity of friendships, and this is where the crux of our exploration begins. When finances flow, the lines between genuine companionship and circumstantial association blur, leaving us with the question: are we cherished for who we are or for the convenience we bring?

As the tide of wealth recedes, the landscape changes. Old allies might drift away, revealing the essence of their presence – one that was more transactional than heartfelt. The allure of shared moments may give way to the glaring reality of convenience-driven bonds, forcing us to discern between those who weather the storm and those who seek fair-weather shelter.

Identifying True Companions: Friends vs. Fair-Weather Friends

Amidst the harsh winds of financial uncertainty, the true value of friendships is laid bare. The fair-weather friends retreat, revealing the resilient companions who are willing to stand by us as our pockets run dry. This revelation, though painful, offers an invaluable lesson in discernment. It teaches us to value those who not only celebrate our highs but also walk alongside us through our lows.

These true friends are the ones who don't shy away from our financial struggles. They stay when the lavish dinners and extravagant outings give way to budget-conscious choices. Their loyalty transcends economic conditions, underlining that the worth of a friendship lies not in the abundance of material resources but in the richness of shared experiences, laughter, and mutual support.

The Awkward Silence: When Money Becomes the Elephant in the Room

Financial adversity also brings with it a palpable awkwardness – the silence that looms when the topic of money becomes the elephant in the room. Conversations that once flowed freely now encounter hushed tones and avoided gazes. Yet, within this unease lies an opportunity for profound growth.

By addressing money-related conversations head-on, we break the shackles of societal taboos. These dialogues, however uncomfortable, create bridges of understanding and compassion. They shatter the illusion of idealized friendships that are unscathed by life's trials, fostering an environment where authenticity can flourish.

Empathy in Action: Stories of Friends Who Stand Strong in the Face of Hardship:

The heart of "Unmasking Friendships: When Pockets Run Dry" is illuminated by stories of courage, kindness, and empathy in the face of financial adversity. Tales of friends who step up, who offer support not as a favor but as an extension of their love, grace the pages. These stories depict the beauty of friendships stripped of materialism, where the currency of empathy holds more weight than a full wallet.

Through anecdotes that span continents and cultures, the book underscores the universality of human emotions in times of need. It is in these stories that we find solace, inspiration, and a gentle reminder that true friendships, when unmasked, shine even more brightly.

Rebuilding Trust: Nurturing Friendships After Weathering Financial Storms

As we journey through these reflections and stories, the path forward becomes clearer. The book gently guides us toward rebuilding trust, nurturing friendships, and forging stronger connections. It encourages us to value authenticity over appearances, to embrace vulnerability, and to seek growth in our relationships even when the landscape is barren.

"Unmasking Friendships: When Pockets Run Dry" is a testament to the resilience of human connections. It is an exploration of the complexities that emerge when wealth fades, revealing the strength that lies within us to navigate these complexities. It reminds us that beneath the surface, friendships stand as a testament to our shared humanity, capable of withstanding the storms of circumstance.

As we turn the final pages, we're invited to reevaluate our own friendships, to question the true nature of our alliances, and to embrace the beauty of authentic connections that transcend the boundaries of materialism. For when we unmask friendships, when pockets run dry, we uncover the profound riches of empathy, compassion, and the enduring bonds that make life truly meaningful.

Tips for Recognizing True Friends: Observe Them Closely in Their Interactions with Family and Relatives. These relationships serve as the bedrock of their lives. If they exhibit kindness and consideration towards their family and relatives, and if they provide support during times of financial difficulty, you can have unwavering faith in their character. On the other hand, if they fail to support their own Foundations, it's apparent that you are merely a temporary convenience. When you possess wealth, they seek your company; but as soon as your resources dwindle, truth becomes evident and you grasp the implications, you'll come to realize what lies ahead: when your pockets run dry, friendships can transform into adversaries.

Chapter 4

A Difficult Journey: From Prosperity to Poverty

In the tapestry of life, transitions can be as formidable as they are transformative. In "Shadows of Change," we delve into an odyssey where abundance dissolves, and prosperity gives way to stark adversity. Join us as we unravel the story of a soul grappling with the uncharted territories of financial turmoil.

In a world where allies were once aplenty, the sudden shift from comfort to destitution casts a pall over familiar faces. "Shadows of Change" portrays the stark reality that arises when your pocketbook is devoid of fortune. Friends, once seemingly steadfast, fade like mirages in the desert, revealing the harsh truth that allegiances are often tethered to material wealth.

But adversity births a new perspective. In the crucible of scarcity, one's resilience shines. "Shadows of Change" paints a vivid picture of how enemies, too, emerge from the depths of envy and mistrust, adding layers of complexity to an already challenging journey.

Through the protagonist's eyes, we traverse a terrain where judgment and compassion dance a delicate tango. The once affluent life becomes a distant echo, replaced by an unexpected camaraderie with fellow travelers who've endured similar trials. As the protagonist navigates the treacherous path, they unearth the strength to forge alliances built on shared experiences rather than fleeting riches.

"Shadows of Change" is an exploration of the human spirit's capacity to adapt and rebuild. It speaks to the resilience that awakens within when the illusion of security is shattered. Join us on this expedition from opulence to insufficiency, where friends, relatives crumble like brittle leaves, and enmities arise like shadows in the dusk. As you turn each page, be prepared to confront the dichotomy of human nature when tested by the crucible of circumstance.

In this saga of transformation, you will witness the emergence of an indomitable force—an evolution of self that transcends the temporal, reminding us that while fortune may falter, the spirit endures. The journey awaits, so let us embark on this compelling narrative together.

Once upon a time, in the bustling city Jhapa of Nepal, lived a man named Ram. He was a beacon of opulence, surrounded by luxuries and comfort. A thriving business empire had granted him wealth beyond measure, yet he lived his days carefree. Money flowed like a river, and Ram reveled in a world of indulgence, ignoring the shadows lurking at the edges of his existence.

In Nepal every street, Ram's name was synonymous with grandeur. His parties were legendary, his possessions were enviable, and his heart was as untouched by the struggles of the world, he didn't care about anything in the world because he had a lot of property.

Ram's life of abundance knew no bounds until one fateful day, when the tides of fortune took a treacherous turn. A series of unexpected events unfolded, unraveling the foundation of his empire. As swiftly as a storm cloud gathers, Ram found himself spiraling from the pinnacle of prosperity to the abyss of poverty.

The once-gilded walls of his mansion were replaced by the harsh reality of a modest dwelling, and the echoes of laughter were replaced by the silence of struggle. Ram's wealth had dissolved like morning mist. As the shadows of change cast their heavy shroud, Ram confronted a world he had never seen—the world he had once turned a blind eye to. Amid the struggle for survival, he encountered the very faces he had chosen to ignore—the poor, the needy, the marginalized.

Their resilience and unity in adversity spoke volumes, igniting a spark within Ram. In the heart of destitution, Ram discovered an understanding that had eluded him in his days of plenty. He experienced firsthand the value of a single coin earned through sweat and sacrifice, the power of frugality, and the possibilities that lay dormant within the judicious use of resources.

Ram's transformation was profound. When he was rich, he didn't care about poor people. He used to make fun of their poverty. But now he began to mend relationships, not with grand gestures, but with heartfelt apologies and humble efforts to make amends. He worked diligently, learning trades and skills that would keep his family afloat. With each sunrise, he witnessed the dawn of a new perspective—one that appreciated the simplest joys, understood the weight of responsibility, and recognized the potential of perseverance.

From the shadows of change emerged a Ram who had been humbled by circumstances yet had risen with a newfound strength. The story of his journey, from a man who once cared for nothing to one who cared for everything, resonated through the street of Nepal. Ram's legacy became a beacon of hope and a reminder that even the most radiant stars could be eclipsed by the shadows, only to emerge stronger and more resilient on the other side.

Understanding how success materializes and comprehending the mechanics of financial discipline are crucial. It involves diligently working in silence and refraining from sharing your future plans until you've achieved success. Once you reach your dreams or goals, it's essential not to keep them hidden. Instead, utilize your experience to aid others on their journeys.

If you attain your goals yet remain silent about them, it might not genuinely be your accomplishment. Reflect on the story of Ram mentioned earlier. In his wealth, he exhibited a disregard for the poor, even mocking them due to his negative money mindset.

However, when the winds of change swept through his life, Ram's perception transformed. He recognized the significance of family, friends, relatives, and financial discipline. This newfound understanding positioned him for prospective success, not only benefiting himself but also those around him.

Achieving success and accumulating wealth isn't the most remarkable feat. True distinction arises from sharing prosperity and enriching the lives of others. When someone's life undergoes positive transformation due to your actions, that's an exceptional achievement.

Once your influence fosters prosperity in others, you can genuinely label yourself a successful individual, both internally and externally. Becoming a catalyst for others' prosperity and life improvements solidifies your success from within your heart and outwardly to the world.

Chapter 5

Defeating Self-Doubt and Depression with "The Enemy Within"

In "The Enemy Within: Navigating Self-Doubt and Depression in the Face of Adversity," we delve into the profound connection between internal struggles and external challenges, such as financial hardship and social isolation. This book serves as a guiding light for those grappling with the dual adversaries of self-doubt and depression when compounded by the overwhelming weight of financial constraints and a perceived lack of support. Through a fusion of personal narratives, psychological insights, and pragmatic tools, readers are invited to unravel the complex web of emotions that can arise when faced with the scarcity of resources and potential social estrangement. By addressing the intertwined nature of these challenges,

"The Enemy Within" offers not only solace but also strategies to transcend these obstacles. This book empowers individuals to rewrite their outlook, fostering resilience, and nurturing self-belief, even in the most trying circumstances. Through 'The Enemy Within,' I articulate my personal perspective on overcoming self-doubt and depression, drawing from my own experiences that can be distilled into three key points."

1. Fighting the Demons of Self-Worth:
Conquering Self-Worth Amidst Financial Strain and Perceived Hostility," we embark on a transformative exploration of the intricate dance between self-worth, financial limitations, and the fear of social alienation. This book stands as a beacon of guidance for those navigating the tumultuous intersection of inner demons and external challenges, particularly the paralyzing fear that financial scarcity breeds contempt from others.

Through a fusion of personal anecdotes, psychological revelations, and actionable strategies, readers are invited to unravel the layers of their own self-perception and their response to the world's perceived judgment.

"Defying Shadows" not only sheds light on the often-hidden nexus of self-worth and financial hardship but also equips individuals with the tools to reclaim their narrative. By embracing their intrinsic value and learning to navigate the labyrinth of human interactions, readers can emerge from this journey with renewed confidence, resilience, and an unshakeable sense of self-worth, regardless of external circumstances.

2. Overcoming Depression in the Face of Adversity:

During the daunting landscape characterized by financial scarcity and the perceived enmity of others, this book delves into the profound journey of 'Overcoming Depression in the Face of Adversity.' Through a tapestry of personal triumphs, psychological insights, and practical strategies, readers are guided through the intricate process of transcending depression while confronting the dual challenges of economic constraints and social skepticism.

By exploring the intricate interplay between these adversities and the internal struggle of depression, this book serves as a compass for those seeking resilience and hope. With each turn of the page, individuals discover the power to reshape their mindset, cultivate self-compassion, and forge an unbreakable spirit capable of navigating life's harshest trials.

'Overcoming Depression in the Face of Adversity' offers a roadmap to reclaiming one's mental well-being, finding light within darkness, and emerging stronger in the face of overwhelming odds.

3. Building Mental Stability and Resilience:
Within the challenging context of financial adversity and the pervasive fear of facing hostility from others, this book illuminates the path to 'Building Mental Stability and Resilience.' Through a comprehensive blend of personal narratives, psychological insights, and actionable strategies, readers are invited on a transformative journey towards cultivating unwavering inner strength. This book serves as a steadfast guide, helping individuals navigate the intricate intersection of external hardships and the fragility of mental well-being.

By unraveling the complexities of building resilience in the face of scarcity and skepticism, readers learn to fortify their minds against the storms of life. With each chapter, they discover the tools to foster stability, nurture self-belief, and construct a resilient foundation capable of weathering any adversity. 'Building Mental Stability and Resilience' empowers individuals to forge a path towards mental equilibrium, illuminating the way to thrive during challenging circumstances.

Chapter 6

"Harmony of Purpose: Cultivating Integrity and Abundance in Life's Melody"

In the intricate tapestry of every sector, one finds the dual specters of leadership/management, illuminated by the stark contrast between virtue and vice. Through the corridors of power and across the landscapes of industry, the narrative unfolds—of leaders/managers, both righteous and unscrupulous. It is a tale as old as time, where the virtuous leaders blaze like meteors across the sky, casting their brilliant influence on the realms they touch, only to fade into obscurity all too soon.

Meanwhile, the unscrupulous managers, like weeds in fertile soil, seem to thrive, ascending the hierarchy with unsettling ease, their tenacity affording them high seats of influence.

Yet, amid this ever-shifting tableau of ambition, there emerges a resounding truth—a truth that defies the fleeting nature of leadership and the transient allure of shortcuts. This truth revolves around the imperative of moral rectitude, the profound significance of ethical conduct, and the enduring impact of actions rooted in integrity.

In a world where the pursuit of wealth is an undeniable facet of existence, let it be a pursuit bound by legality, a path carved with patience, a journey that resonates with one's unique circumstances. The allure of swift gains through dubious means may whisper seductively, but wisdom shuns such a treacherous path.

As we traverse the realms of daily labor or entrepreneurial fervor, let goodness be our constant companion. Let discernment guide our judgments, allowing us to perceive the true essence of those who cross our paths. For while wealth may be a coveted prize, it must never eclipse the triumph of character. In a world enamored by opulence, let us remember that wealth is but an ephemeral companion on the journey of life—a companion that, when our time comes to depart, shall remain behind.

Consider, for a moment, the legacy that transcends mortal boundaries. A legacy not measured solely in material abundance, but in the lives positively touched, the trails of benevolence blazed, and the ripples of kindness that extend far beyond our years. As dawn breaks, illuminating the canvas of a new day, pause to express gratitude for the gift of life's continuation. In the solitude of prayer, commune with the divine, anchoring your aspirations in goodness. Nourish your body, invigorate your spirit, and let music be the language that bridges the earthly and the ethereal.

Yet, it is in our capacity to assist that the essence of humanity finds its purest expression. Extend your hand to those in need, not as an obligation, but as a testament to the compassion within. Guide them not only through their trials, but also down the path of virtuous conduct. For a life enriched by goodwill leaves an indelible mark, etching itself into the hearts of those graced by its warmth. In weaving together, the strands of wealth and virtue, we attain a state beyond mere affluence—it is an embodiment of timeless values, an elevation of the human spirit.

As we venture forth in entrepreneurial pursuit, remember that even the humblest beginnings bear the seeds of resilience. Jobs, those vessels of livelihood, pale in comparison to the narrative woven through the art of entrepreneurship. For job titles may be revoked, but the legacy of a well-nurtured venture stands steadfast. In this grand tapestry of existence, the dichotomy between leadership's light and darkness becomes apparent. The journey invites us to ascend or descend, to radiate virtue or to wither under the cloak of vice. The choice, in the end, is uniquely ours to make.

So, let our legacy be etched not only in the monuments of prosperity, but in the hearts of humanity. To blend wealth and goodness is to compose a symphony that resonates across generations, a legacy that lives on, a testament to a life that dared to shine brightly, both rich and good.

Chapter 7

Family can sometimes be your worst critic.

In a world where Family is often seen as the unbreakable thread, the unwavering support, the refuge in times of trouble. Yet, paradoxically, it is within the confines of the familial circle that the echoes of empty pockets can sometimes resonate most sharply. Financial hardship, like an unexpected tempest, can disrupt the harmony of family life, turning those who should be your staunchest allies into unwitting adversaries, poised to critique your every move.

The sound of empty pockets, those telltale hollowness's where once there were coins jingling with promise, can reverberate through the heart of family relationships. It is precisely when the coffers run dry, and the weight of unpaid bills hangs heavy, that familial judgments can cut the deepest. In the eyes of those who share your bloodline, the absence of wealth can often translate into the presence of unwelcome scrutiny. The echoing clinks of criticism can mingle with the silence of scarcity, creating a discordant symphony that punctuates the struggles of daily life.

The very people who should provide solace in moments of financial turmoil sometimes become the inadvertent purveyors of criticism. Their intentions may be rooted in concern, but the unsolicited advice, the raised eyebrows, the not-so-subtle insinuations can feel like an assault on one's self-worth. As the bank account dwindles, so too can the sense of autonomy and dignity, eroded by well-meaning but ill-timed opinions from those who mean the most.

The emptiness of one's pockets can become a mirror reflecting the judgments of family members, amplifying their voices until they seem inescapable. It is in these moments that family dynamics, once marked by love and acceptance, can warp under the pressure of financial strain.

What was once an unbreakable bond can feel tenuous, stretched thin by the weight of expectations and critiques. The warm hearth of home can become a crucible where familial relationships are tested, sometimes to their limits.

There is a vulnerability in financial hardship that exposes the fault lines in even the closest-knit families. The money that once flowed freely now trickles through clenched fists, and with it, the assurance that family should be a safe haven. Instead, it can become a place where every decision is dissected, every misstep magnified, every choice questioned. The echoes of empty pockets can lead to arguments, misunderstandings, and a palpable sense of disconnection.

Yet, within this turbulent sea of familial judgment, there exists the potential for growth, for understanding, for resilience. For it is precisely during these moments of financial trial that the true strength of familial bonds is tested. It is an opportunity to communicate, to bridge gaps, to reevaluate priorities. It is a reminder that family, in all its imperfect complexity, is composed of individuals with their own fears, hopes, and insecurities.

In the echoes of empty pockets, one can find not only criticism but also compassion. Amidst the judgment, there is the potential for empathy. And within the turmoil, there lies the possibility of deeper connection. For family, even when serving as the harshest critic, can also be the source of enduring love and support, the refuge in the storm, and the unwavering thread that, despite the strains, weaves the fabric of our lives together.

Chapter 8

How to handle peer jealousy and enmity.

In the echo chamber of today's world, where materialism often overshadows genuine human connections, it's no surprise that peer jealousy and enmity can rear their ugly heads. As we navigate the tumultuous waters of life, especially when our pockets feel emptier than those around us, it becomes crucial to understand and manage these complex emotions. This guide explores how to handle peer jealousy and enmity in the echoes of empty pockets.

Self-Reflection and Gratitude:
The first step in dealing with peer jealousy and enmity is to turn inward. Reflect on your own values, goals, and accomplishments. Cultivate a sense of gratitude for what you have achieved so far, no matter how small it may seem. Remember that wealth is not solely measured in monetary terms; it encompasses health, happiness, and relationships as well.

Empathy and Understanding:
Jealousy often arises from a lack of understanding. Try to put yourself in your peer's shoes. Understand that their journey, experiences, and circumstances are different from yours. This empathy can soften the edges of envy and foster a more compassionate perspective.

Communicate Openly:
Effective communication is key to resolving conflicts stemming from jealousy or enmity. Approach your peers with an open heart and a willingness to listen. Express your feelings calmly and honestly, and encourage them to do the same. Often, talking things out can lead to a better understanding and the resolution of misunderstandings.

Set Boundaries:
Sometimes, peer jealousy and enmity can become toxic. In such cases, it's essential to set clear boundaries to protect your well-being. Limit your exposure to negative influences and surround yourself with supportive friends and family. Recognize when a relationship may no longer serve your best interests and be prepared to let go.

Focus on Personal Growth:
Instead of dwelling on the success of others, channel your energy into personal growth and self-improvement. Use your empty pockets as a source of motivation to work harder, learn more, and achieve your goals. Success born from your efforts will bring a sense of fulfillment that no material possession can provide.

Avoid Social Comparison:
Comparing yourself to others is a surefire way to fuel jealousy and enmity. Remember that everyone's path is unique, and social media often presents an idealized version of reality. Limit your exposure to such comparisons and focus on your journey, celebrating your small wins along the way.

Seek Professional Help:
If jealousy and enmity are overwhelming and affecting your mental health, consider seeking professional help. A therapist or counselor can provide guidance and strategies to cope with these emotions, helping you develop healthier ways of dealing with peer jealousy.

Cultivate Positive Relationships:
Surround yourself with positive, like-minded individuals who support your goals and aspirations. Healthy friendships can provide a strong support system, offering encouragement and understanding during challenging times.

Practice Self-Care:
Taking care of your physical and emotional well-being is crucial when dealing with jealousy and enmity. Incorporate self-care routines into your daily life, such as exercise, meditation, and hobbies that bring you joy. These activities can help alleviate stress and boost your self-esteem.

Keep Your Perspective:
In the grand scheme of life, material wealth and possessions often pale in comparison to the richness of genuine connections, personal growth, and inner happiness. Remember that the echoes of empty pockets can be drowned out by the harmonious melody of a fulfilling life.

Conclusion:
Dealing with peer jealousy and enmity in the echoes of empty pockets requires self-awareness, empathy, and resilience. By focusing on personal growth, nurturing positive relationships, and practicing self-care, you can rise above the noise of envy and cultivate a life filled with meaning and contentment. Embrace your unique journey and let it be your guide toward a fulfilling and joyful existence.

Chapter 9

Making Ends Meet: Practical Advice for Financial Stability

In today's fast-paced and ever-changing world, many people find it challenging to make ends meet financially. Whether you're facing unexpected expenses, dealing with a limited income, or striving to save for the future, practical strategies can help you achieve financial stability. This guide offers valuable advice to assist you in managing your finances and making ends meet.

Create a Budget

The cornerstone of financial stability is creating a budget. Start by tracking your income and expenses. Categorize your spending to identify areas where you can cut back or eliminate unnecessary costs. A well-structured budget allows you to allocate your income effectively and plan for future financial goals.

Prioritize Essential Expenses

When money is tight, prioritize essential expenses such as housing, utilities, groceries, and transportation. Ensure that these necessities are covered before allocating funds to discretionary spending. This approach ensures that your basic needs are met, even during financially challenging times.

Emergency Fund

Building an emergency fund is crucial for handling unexpected expenses without derailing your financial stability. Aim to save at least three to six months' worth of living expenses in a separate savings account. This safety net can provide peace of mind and prevent you from accumulating debt in emergencies.

Reduce Debt

High-interest debt, such as credit card balances, can be a significant obstacle to making ends meet. Develop a plan to pay off existing debts by allocating extra funds toward them each month. Consider consolidating high-interest debts or negotiating with creditors to lower interest rates.

Increase Income

Finding ways to boost your income can make it easier to make ends meet. Look for part-time or freelance work, explore gig economy opportunities, or invest in skills that can lead to a higher-paying job. Increasing your income provides more financial flexibility and accelerates your path to financial stability.

Cut Unnecessary Expenses

Trimming non-essential expenses is an effective way to free up more money in your budget. Evaluate your discretionary spending, such as dining out, entertainment, or subscription services. Identify areas where you can cut back and redirect those funds toward your financial goals.

Plan for Retirement

While it may seem distant, planning for retirement is essential for long-term financial stability. Contribute to retirement accounts like a 401(k) or IRA, especially if your employer offers matching contributions. The earlier you start saving for retirement, the more time your investments have to grow.

Shop Smart

Optimize your spending by adopting savvy shopping habits. Look for discounts, use coupons, and compare prices before making purchases. Consider buying generic brands, and avoid impulse buying. These practices can help you make the most of your budget.

Financial Education

Invest in your financial education to improve your money management skills. Books, courses, and online resources can provide valuable insights into budgeting, investing, and personal finance. Knowledge is a powerful tool for achieving financial stability.

Seek Professional Guidance

If you're struggling to manage your finances, consider seeking advice from a financial advisor or credit counselor. They can help you create a personalized plan to address your specific financial challenges and work toward making ends meet.

Conclusion

Achieving financial stability and making ends meet is a journey that requires discipline, determination, and the application of practical strategies. By creating a budget, prioritizing essential expenses, building an emergency fund, reducing debt, increasing income, and planning for the future, you can improve your financial well-being. Remember that small, consistent steps toward financial stability can lead to significant improvements in your financial situation over time.

Chapter 10

Embracing change and seizing opportunities.

Change is a force that can sometimes feel like an unwelcome guest, especially when it accompanies empty pockets and financial hardship. But, paradoxically, it is often in these very echoes of empty pockets that we find the most profound opportunities for transformation and growth. In this narrative, we will explore the intricate relationship between embracing change and seizing opportunities, even when the pockets seem devoid of resources.

Financial Change and Its Impact

Change, when it relates to our financial circumstances, can be particularly challenging. Job loss, economic downturns, or unexpected expenses can leave us grappling with empty pockets and uncertainty about our future. Yet, it's precisely in such times that the potential for personal and financial evolution is most ripe.

The Nature of Change

Change is a constant companion throughout our lives. It can manifest in various forms, from personal transitions like career shifts and relationships to global phenomena such as technological advancements and societal shifts. Yet, in the midst of change, we often encounter a sense of emptiness, an uncertainty that can be both unsettling and exhilarating.

Embracing Resourcefulness

To embrace change amidst empty pockets is to cultivate resourcefulness. It involves a mindset shift from dwelling on what's lacking to focusing on what can be created from the resources at hand. Resourcefulness encourages us to find innovative solutions, explore new avenues, and leverage our existing skills and networks.

The Power of Adaptation

Change forces us to adapt, and in the realm of finance, adaptation often involves budgeting, prioritizing, and making tough choices. It's a time to reassess our financial goals and reevaluate what truly matters to us. Empty pockets can be a catalyst for adopting a simpler and more intentional lifestyle.

Entrepreneurial Spirit

Seizing opportunities in the face of financial change can mean exploring entrepreneurship or side hustles. An empty pocket can become the catalyst for a new business idea, a freelance career, or a creative endeavor. In these pursuits, we discover the power of our own ingenuity and the potential for financial independence.

Learning from Financial Setbacks

Financial setbacks can be painful, but they also offer valuable lessons. They teach us resilience, frugality, and the importance of saving for the future. The echoes of empty pockets remind us to be prepared and to value financial security, once we regain it.

Investing in Knowledge and Skills

Change often necessitates acquiring new knowledge and skills. Investing in education or training, even when resources are limited, can pay dividends in the long run. It's an opportunity to increase one's earning potential and open doors to new career possibilities.

Community and Collaboration

During times of financial change, communities often come together to support one another. Embracing change can mean reaching out for help and forming partnerships. Collaboration can create opportunities that were otherwise inaccessible, as it leverages the collective resources and expertise of a group.

Creating Financial Resilience

Seizing opportunities in the echoes of empty pockets involves a commitment to financial resilience. This resilience can be built through saving, investing wisely, and diversifying income streams. It ensures that we are better equipped to weather future financial storms.

A Shift in Values

Change often prompts a shift in our values. We may come to prioritize experiences over possessions, relationships over material wealth, and personal growth over financial success. Embracing this shift can lead to a more fulfilling and purpose-driven life, regardless of our financial circumstances.

"In this chapter, I've presented the information in brief points to maintain engagement and clarity, as I aim to avoid boring the reader."

Conclusion:

Embracing change and seizing opportunities in the echoes of empty pockets is a testament to the human spirit's resilience and adaptability. It's a reminder that even when our financial resources are scarce, our capacity for growth and transformation remains abundant. By cultivating resourcefulness, learning from setbacks, and embracing the opportunities that arise, we not only navigate financial change but also thrive in its wake. In the echoes of empty pockets, we discover our own capacity to create, adapt, and succeed, demonstrating that true wealth lies not only in our bank accounts but in our ability to embrace change and seize the opportunities it presents.

Chapter 11

The Path to Empowerment: Moving from Conflict to Unity.

In a world often marked by division and discord, the journey towards empowerment takes center stage, illuminating a path that leads from conflict to unity. Empowerment, in its essence, is not merely a destination but a continuous voyage that transcends personal, societal, and global boundaries.

This transformative journey calls upon us to harness our inner strength, resolve conflicts, and embrace unity, ultimately empowering ourselves and those around us.

Empowerment begins with self-discovery. To embark on this path, we must first understand ourselves, our values, and our aspirations. In doing so, we become more attuned to our strengths and weaknesses, enabling us to navigate life's challenges with clarity and purpose. As we peel back the layers of our identity, we gain a deeper sense of self-awareness, laying the foundation for personal growth and empowerment.

Conflict, though often perceived as a hindrance, is an integral part of the empowerment journey. It is through conflict that we learn valuable lessons about ourselves and others. Conflict tests our resilience and challenges us to develop effective communication skills and emotional intelligence. When approached with an open heart and mind, conflict can be a catalyst for personal growth and transformation.

One of the key aspects of empowerment is the ability to resolve conflicts constructively. Instead of viewing conflicts as roadblocks, we can see them as opportunities for dialogue, understanding, and compromise. Conflict resolution fosters empathy and cooperation, paving the way for unity. It requires active listening, empathy, and a commitment to finding common ground. When individuals, communities, and nations engage in productive conflict resolution, they move one step closer to unity.

Unity is the ultimate destination on the path to empowerment. It is a state of harmony, where diverse individuals and groups come together, recognizing their shared humanity and interconnectedness. Unity does not erase differences; instead, it celebrates them as a source of strength and richness. In a world that often accentuates divisions, unity becomes a powerful antidote, fostering tolerance, collaboration, and peace.

The journey towards empowerment is not without its challenges. Along the way, we may encounter resistance, setbacks, and moments of self-doubt. Yet, these trials are integral to our growth. They teach us resilience and the importance of perseverance. Empowerment is not a linear path; it is a dynamic and evolving process that requires continuous self-reflection and adaptation.

As we progress along the path to empowerment, we discover that it is not a solitary journey. Empowerment is interwoven with the empowerment of others. When we empower ourselves, we are better equipped to uplift those around us. We become agents of positive change, inspiring others to embark on their own journeys towards empowerment. Together, we create a ripple effect that can transform families, communities, and societies.

In the quest for empowerment, education and awareness play pivotal roles. Knowledge empowers us by expanding our horizons and enabling us to make informed choices. Education fosters critical thinking, creativity, and innovation, equipping us to address complex challenges and forge a brighter future. By promoting education and awareness, we empower individuals and communities to make conscious, positive choices that lead to unity and collective empowerment.

In conclusion, the path to empowerment is a profound journey that leads from conflict to unity. It is a journey of self-discovery, conflict resolution, and personal growth. Empowerment not only transforms individuals but also has the potential to unite diverse communities and nations. As we navigate this path, let us remember that empowerment is not a solitary pursuit; it is a shared endeavor that requires empathy, understanding, and a commitment to building a more harmonious and empowered world for all.

Chapter 11

"Debit vs. Credit: Unveiling the Difference"

Debit and Credit Essentials for Financial Beginners

Financial literacy is a cornerstone of personal financial success. Understanding the fundamentals of debit and credit is crucial for anyone embarking on their journey to financial stability. These concepts, often seen as the building blocks of personal finance, are not only practical but also empower individuals to make informed financial decisions. In this section, we will delve deep into the essentials of debit and credit, demystifying these terms and providing insights for financial beginners.

Debit vs. Credit: What's the Difference?

At its core, the distinction between debit and credit lies in how money flows in and out of your accounts. A debit transaction represents the removal of funds from your account, essentially reducing your available balance. On the other hand, a credit transaction is the addition of funds to your account, increasing your available balance. Understanding this basic concept is key to managing your finances effectively.

The Power of Debit Cards

For many financial beginners, debit cards are the first financial tool they encounter. These cards are typically linked to your checking account, allowing you to make purchases or withdraw cash up to the available balance. Debit cards offer convenience and security. You can use them for everyday expenses like groceries, gas, and online shopping. However, it's essential to keep track of your spending and your account balance to avoid overdraft fees.

One of the advantages of using a debit card is that it discourages overspending. Since you can only spend what's available in your account, there's no risk of accumulating credit card debt. This makes debit cards a practical choice for those who want to maintain strict control over their spending.

Understanding Credit Cards

Credit cards, on the other hand, work differently. When you make a purchase with a credit card, you're essentially borrowing money from the card issuer, with the promise to pay it back later. The credit card company extends you a line of credit, which has a predetermined limit. As you make purchases, your available credit decreases. It's important to remember that using a credit card isn't the same as spending your own money. It's a form of short-term borrowing.

Credit cards come with a monthly billing cycle. At the end of the cycle, you receive a statement outlining your charges. To avoid interest charges, it's crucial to pay your statement balance in full by the due date. If you only make a partial payment, the remaining balance will accrue interest, potentially leading to credit card debt.

Building Credit History

One significant advantage of responsible credit card usage is the opportunity to build a positive credit history. Your credit history is a record of your borrowing and repayment behavior. It plays a critical role in your financial life, impacting your ability to secure loans, mortgages, and even job opportunities.

Financial beginners often start with a limited or nonexistent credit history, making it challenging to qualify for loans or credit cards with favorable terms. By responsibly using a credit card, you can begin building a positive credit history. Timely payments and responsible credit management demonstrate to creditors that you are a reliable borrower.

Debit Card Safety and Security

While debit cards offer convenience, it's essential to be mindful of security. If your debit card is lost or stolen, unauthorized individuals could access your funds. To mitigate this risk, promptly report any lost or stolen cards to your bank. Most banks offer fraud protection programs to safeguard your account.

Another aspect of debit card security is protecting your Personal Identification Number (PIN). Never share your PIN with anyone, and when using an ATM or making a purchase, shield the keypad to prevent others from seeing your PIN.

Responsible Credit Card Usage

Responsible credit card usage is vital for avoiding debt and building good credit. Here are some key practices for financial beginners:

Pay on Time: Always pay your credit card bill on time to avoid late fees and interest charges. Set up reminders or automatic payments to ensure punctual payments.

Stay Below the Credit Limit: Avoid maxing out your credit card. It's advisable to keep your credit utilization—the percentage of your credit limit you're using—below 30%.

Pay in Full: Whenever possible, pay your credit card balance in full each month. This not only prevents interest charges but also helps build a positive credit history.

Monitor Your Statements: Regularly review your credit card statements to identify any unauthorized charges or errors. Promptly report discrepancies to your card issuer.

Budget Wisely: Use your credit card as a tool to manage your finances, not as a source of additional income. Create a budget and stick to it to avoid overspending.

Debit or Credit: Which Should You Use?

The choice between using a debit or credit card depends on your financial goals and preferences. Debit cards offer simplicity and can help you control spending, making them a suitable choice for everyday expenses. On the other hand, credit cards provide a valuable opportunity to build credit history when used responsibly. They also offer benefits such as rewards programs, purchase protection, and travel perks.

Many financial experts recommend using both types of cards strategically. Use your debit card for daily expenses and as a budgeting tool, while using a credit card for larger purchases or transactions where credit card benefits are advantageous. This approach allows you to enjoy the best of both worlds while managing your finances effectively.

Conclusion

In conclusion, understanding the basics of debit and credit is essential for anyone starting their journey to financial literacy. Debit cards offer convenience and control over your spending, while credit cards, when used responsibly, can help you build credit history and offer valuable benefits. As a financial beginner, the key is to use these financial tools wisely, setting the foundation for a secure and prosperous financial future. By mastering the essentials of debit and credit, you can make informed financial decisions and pave the way for a more secure and prosperous financial future.

Chapter 13

Embracing Resilience: Transforming Adversity into Strength.

In the echoes of empty pockets, where scarcity meets struggle, and dreams seem distant, resilience emerges as the guiding light—a beacon of hope that transforms adversity into strength. In the world of limited resources, both material and emotional, the journey of embracing resilience becomes an art, a philosophy, and a lifeline. we will embark on a profound exploration of how can resonate with the resilience of the human spirit.

Resilience Amidst Scarcity

Imagine a life where the economic tides are ever turbulent, where the wallet is often barren, and where uncertainty looms like a dark cloud. It is in these moments that the true essence of resilience is tested and revealed. Resilience is not the absence of adversity but rather the ability to thrive despite it. It's a quality that resides deep within us, waiting to be nurtured and harnessed, especially when financial resources are scarce.

The Resilient Mindset

Resilience begins with a shift in mindset. Instead of viewing empty pockets as a symbol of defeat, the resilient mind perceives them as a blank canvas, an opportunity for transformation. In the face of economic hardship, resilient individuals do not surrender to despair but rather embrace hope and determination.

They recognize that while they may lack financial abundance, they possess the wealth of creativity, resourcefulness, and grit. This shift in perspective empowers them to chart new paths, explore uncharted territories, and turn adversity into a catalyst for change.

Lessons from Adversity

Embracing resilience is not about ignoring the hardships but embracing them as valuable teachers. Every empty pocket and financial setback have lessons to offer. It teaches frugality, prudent spending, and the importance of saving for a rainy day. These lessons, when embraced, can transform empty pockets into a university of financial wisdom.

Moreover, adversity instills empathy and compassion. Those who have experienced financial struggles are often more understanding and willing to help others in similar situations. Thus, adversity becomes a bridge connecting people in their shared experiences.

Resourceful Adaptation

Resourcefulness is the hallmark of resilient individuals in the echoes of empty pockets. They adapt to their circumstances, seeking innovative solutions to everyday challenges. From budgeting techniques to (Do it yourself) DIY repairs, they find creative ways to make the most of what they have. Resourcefulness is not limited to tangible resources alone. It extends to the ability to tap into personal strengths, knowledge, and skills. In the absence of financial wealth, one discovers the wealth within themselves—a wealth that is priceless and sustainable.

Building Financial Resilience

Financial resilience is not merely about surviving paycheck to paycheck but about creating a sturdy financial foundation. This involves prudent financial planning, saving for emergencies, and investing in one's financial education. In the echoes of empty pockets, financial resilience is the compass that guides individuals towards a more secure future.

Community Support

In the journey of embracing resilience, one does not walk alone. Communities that face economic challenges often come together with a collective spirit of resilience. They create support networks, share resources, and lift each other up during tough times. In these communities, the strength of resilience is multiplied, and adversity becomes a stepping stone to unity and growth.

The Power of Perseverance

Empty pockets can be disheartening, but they do not define one's worth or potential. Resilience is the determination to persevere despite the odds. It's the unwavering belief that tomorrow can be better than today. Through persistent effort, individuals in the echoes of empty pockets can carve out brighter and more prosperous futures for themselves and their families.

Conclusion: The Symphony of Resilience

It is a melody composed of hope, adaptability, resourcefulness, and determination. Adversity may cast shadows, but resilience illuminates the path forward. As we embrace resilience, we learn to dance to the rhythm of life, even when the music seems faint.

Embracing resilience in the echoes of empty pockets is not just a survival strategy; it is a transformational journey. It's about turning limitations into opportunities, scarcity into abundance of spirit, and despair into hope. It's the reminder that in the face of adversity, we have the power to rise, to grow, and to thrive.

As we conclude this exploration, let us remember that the echoes of empty pockets need not drown out our dreams. Instead, they can be the echo that reverberates with the strength of resilience—a strength that can transform not only our financial circumstances but also the very essence of who we are. Embracing resilience is not a choice; it is a testament to the indomitable human spirit that refuses to be defined by empty pockets but instead chooses to define its own destiny.

Chapter 14

Wealth Mastery in the Echoes of Empty Pockets: Navigating Assets, Liabilities, and the Art of Earning Real Money.

In the symphony of financial uncertainty, where empty pockets echo the struggle for stability, understanding the dynamics of assets and liabilities becomes paramount. This journey involves not just accumulating wealth but mastering the art of using money wisely and creating avenues for substantial earnings. we will embark on a comprehensive exploration of the concepts of assets and liabilities, unraveling the intricacies of financial decision-making, and unveiling practical strategies for earning real money in the echoes of empty pockets.

The Foundation: Assets and Liabilities Defined
At the heart of financial literacy lies the fundamental understanding of assets and liabilities. Assets are resources with economic value that are expected to provide future benefits. These can range from real estate and investments to skills and education. On the other hand, liabilities are obligations or debts that require future repayment.

Types of Assets: Building the Wealth Foundation
Tangible Assets: Real estate, vehicles, and precious metals represent tangible assets. These have intrinsic value and the potential for appreciation over time.

Financial Assets: Investments such as stocks, bonds, and mutual funds fall under this category. They can generate income through dividends, interest, or capital gains.

Intangible Assets: Skills, education, and intellectual property contribute to one's earning capacity. These intangible assets enhance personal and professional development.

Liabilities: Managing the Debt Burden.

Good Debt vs. Bad Debt: Not all liabilities are detrimental. Good debt, such as a mortgage for a property that appreciates in value, can contribute to wealth-building. Bad debt, like high-interest consumer loans, can hinder financial progress.

Debt Repayment Strategies: Prioritizing high-interest debt, creating a realistic repayment plan, and negotiating with creditors are effective strategies for managing liabilities.

The Art of Money Management: Leveraging Assets and Mitigating Liabilities

Creating a Financial Blueprint: Budgeting and Saving

Budgeting: Developing a realistic budget help allocate resources effectively, prioritize financial goals, and curb unnecessary expenses.

Emergency Fund: Establishing an emergency fund is a crucial step in financial planning. This reserve provides a safety net during unexpected expenses or income disruptions.

Strategic Use of Debt: Leveraging Assets

Strategic Borrowing: Utilizing low-interest debt for investments with potential returns higher than the borrowing cost can be a strategic move. This could include investing in education or starting a business.

Mortgage as a Wealth-Building Tool: A mortgage for a property with growth potential can be a tool for building equity and long-term wealth.

Investing Wisely: Growing Assets

Diversification: Spreading investments across different asset classes reduces risk. A well-diversified portfolio may include stocks, bonds, real estate, and other investment vehicles.

Long-Term Perspective: Patience is a virtue in investing. Compound interest and the power of time can significantly amplify returns.

Educated Investing: Continuously educating oneself about financial markets, investment instruments, and economic trends is crucial for making informed investment decisions.

Earning Real Money: Strategies for Prosperity in Empty Pockets (Entrepreneurship: The Path to Financial Independence).

Identifying Opportunities: Entrepreneurs thrive by identifying gaps in the market and offering innovative solutions. This could involve turning personal skills or passions into a business venture.

Bootstrapping: Starting small and scaling gradually reduces the financial burden. Many successful businesses began as side ventures while individuals maintained their primary sources of income.

Adaptability: The ability to adapt to market trends and consumer needs is essential for sustained success. This may involve pivoting business models or introducing new products/services.

Freelancing and Side Hustles: Monetizing Skills
Leveraging Skills: Freelancing platforms allow individuals to monetize their skills, whether in writing, graphic design, programming, or other areas.

Building a Side Business: A side hustle can complement existing income streams and, over time, evolve into a primary source of revenue.

Online Marketplaces: Platforms like Etsy, Upwork, and Fiverr provide opportunities to reach a global audience and generate income.

Investing in Education and Skills: The Personal Capital Advantage

Continuous Learning: Acquiring new skills or enhancing existing ones increases employability and opens doors to higher-paying opportunities.

Certifications and Degrees: Investing in relevant certifications or degrees can lead to promotions, career changes, or entrepreneurial ventures.

Real Estate: A Tangible Path to Wealth

Homeownership: While a home is often considered a personal asset, its value can appreciate over time, contributing to long-term wealth.

Real Estate Investment: Acquiring rental properties or participating in real estate investment trusts (REITs) provides opportunities for passive income and capital appreciation.

Overcoming Challenges and Building Resilience Financial Literacy: Empowering Through Knowledge.

Educational Initiatives: Governments, NGOs, and community organizations play a vital role in promoting financial literacy through workshops, seminars, and accessible resources.

Personal Responsibility: Taking charge of one's financial education empowers individuals to make informed decisions and navigate economic challenges.

Resilience in Economic Downturns: Weathering the Storm

Emergency Preparedness: Having a financial contingency plan and emergency fund is crucial for weathering economic downturns.

Adapting to Change: Resilience involves adapting to changing economic landscapes. This may require upskilling, diversifying income streams, or exploring new opportunities.

Community Support: Strengthening Through Solidarity.

Resource Sharing: Communities can foster resilience by creating networks for resource sharing, mutual support, and collaborative economic initiatives.

Entrepreneurial Ecosystems: Supporting local businesses and creating an environment conducive to entrepreneurship can stimulate economic growth within communities.

Conclusion: Mastering the Art of Wealth in Empty Pockets

In the echoes of empty pockets, the journey towards financial mastery is not just about accumulating wealth but understanding the nuanced dance between assets and liabilities. It's about leveraging resources, making strategic financial decisions, and embracing opportunities for real money in the face of adversity.

As we navigate this complex landscape, let us remember that the echoes of empty pockets need not drown our aspirations. Instead, they can serve as the rhythm urging us to master the art of wealth, to turn liabilities into assets, and to carve a path towards financial prosperity in the echoes of financial uncertainty. In the symphony of wealth mastery, let resilience be the melody that guides us through the challenges, transforming empty pockets into a canvas of opportunity and financial empowerment.

Chapter 15

Navigating the Digital Landscape: A Comprehensive Guide to Online Platforms and Entrepreneurial Ventures for Financial Success.

There are numerous online platforms that offer opportunities to generate real money, and the suitability of each platform can depend on your skills, interests, and the amount of time you are willing to invest. Keep in mind that success often requires effort, dedication, and sometimes a learning curve. Here are some legitimate online platforms across various categories:

1. Freelance Work Platforms: a. **Upwork:** Connects freelancers with clients looking for services in writing, graphic design, programming, marketing, and more.
b. **Fiverr:** Offers a platform for freelancers to sell their services, often starting at $5 per gig.

2. **Online Marketplaces:** a. **Etsy:** Ideal for selling handmade or unique products, arts, crafts, and vintage items.
b. **Amazon and eBay:** These platforms allow you to sell a wide range of products, either used or new.

3. **Content Creation Platforms:** a. **YouTube:** Earn money through ads, sponsorships, and channel memberships by creating and uploading videos.
b. **Twitch:** If you're into gaming or creative content, you can earn through subscriptions, donations, and sponsorships.

4. **Online Tutoring and Education:** a. **Chegg Tutors, Tutor.com:** Connect with students for online tutoring in various subjects.
b. **Udemy, Teachable:** Create and sell online courses on platforms that reach a global audience.

5. **Remote Work Platforms:** a. **Remote OK, We Work Remotely:** Job boards specifically focused on remote work opportunities.
b. **Flex Jobs:** Subscription-based service offering curated remote and flexible job listings.

6. **Affiliate Marketing:** a. **Amazon Associates:** Earn commissions by promoting and selling Amazon products through affiliate links.
b. **Click Bank, Share Sale:** Platforms offering a wide range of products for affiliate marketing.

7. **Stock Photography:** a. **Shutterstock, Adobe Stock:** Upload and sell your photos for commercial use. b. **iStock:** Another platform for selling stock photos.

8. **Investing Platforms:** a. **Robinhood, E*TRADE:** Online platforms for stock trading and investing. b. **Wealth front,**
Betterment: Robo-advisors for automated and diversified investing.

9. **Online Surveys and Reviews:** a. **Swagbucks, Inbox Dollars:** Earn money by taking surveys, watching videos, and completing online tasks.
b. **Product Testing Websites:** Platforms like Influencer or Smiley360 provide free products in exchange for reviews.

10. **Remote Freelance Writing:** a. **Text broker, Writer Access:** Platforms connecting writers with clients seeking content.
b. **Medium Partner Program:** Earn money by writing on the medium platform based on reader engagement.

11. **Virtual Assistance and Admin Tasks:** a. **Fancy Hands, Time Etc.:** Platforms where you can offer virtual assistance services.
b. **TaskRabbit:** Connects people who need help with various tasks with skilled individuals.

Consider exploring the various online platforms mentioned above in your free time to see which aligns best with your skills and interests. However, based on my knowledge, the most effective approach is to start your own business, even if it's on a small scale. Initiatives such as opening a tea or coffee shop, a restaurant, or any venture within your capabilities can provide a more sustainable and personally fulfilling path. Starting your own business allows you to exercise creative control, build a brand, and directly engage with your community. It may require initial effort and dedication, but the potential for long-term success and personal satisfaction often outweighs the uncertainties associated with online endeavors.

Remember to approach online opportunities with caution, as there are also scams. Research each platform thoroughly, read reviews, and, if possible, start with smaller commitments before investing more time or money. Success often comes with perseverance, learning, and adapting to the evolving online landscape.

Dear Readers,

Embarking on the journey of "Echoes of Empty Pockets" has been an exploration of profound meanings and silent echoes that resonate within the chambers of our lives. As the author, Samel Karki, I extend my deepest gratitude for allowing these words to find a place in your hearts and minds. Never give up; approach everything with sincerity and passion. May you achieve success in all your endeavors, and may prosperity follow you wherever you go.

This short book delves into the profound tapestry of life, weaving narratives of resilience and the echoes that emanate from the pockets that bear the weight of scarcity.

It is my sincere hope that the pages of this work serve as a source of inspiration, sparking a flame of determination within you. May it encourage you to confront challenges with unwavering strength and discover the latent power within your own story.

In the symphony of life, may these words be a melody that resonates with your aspirations, urging you to pursue your dreams with unyielding focus and dedication. Like the eagle soaring high in the sky, may you navigate the vast expanse of possibilities, and may success be the wind beneath your wings.

Your support and engagement with "Echoes of Empty Pockets" are not just a testament to my journey but a shared exploration of the human experience. If you find yourself with questions or doubts, or if you simply wish to share your thoughts, I am here. Feel free to reach out at the contact details provided below. Let our connection transcend the pages of this book, and may it be a conversation that continues to enrich our lives.

Wishing you all the success, fulfillment, and joy that life has to offer.

Warm regards,
Samel Karki

“Echoes of Empty pockets”

Author: Samel karki

Instagram: @samel.karki.370
Email: samel.karki20@gmail.com

Made in the USA
Las Vegas, NV
21 September 2024

95320779R00059